For Matthew
~ CL

For Sven
~ GH

LITTLE TIGER PRESS
An imprint of Magi Publications
1 The Coda Centre, 189 Munster Road, London SW6 6AW
www.littletigerpress.com

First published in Great Britain 2003
This edition published 2008

Text copyright © Christine Leeson 2003
Illustrations copyright © Gaby Hansen 2003
Christine Leeson and Gaby Hansen have asserted their
rights to be identified as the author and illustrator of this work
under the Copyright, Designs and Patents Act, 1988.

ISBN 978 1 84506 811 0

A CIP catalogue record for this book
is available from the British Library

Printed in China

1 3 5 7 9 10 8 6 4 2

MOLLY and the STORM

Christine Leeson　　Gaby Hansen

LITTLE TIGER PRESS
London

It was the first sunny day after weeks and
weeks of rain.
"Can we go out to play, Mum?" asked Molly
  Mouse, dancing in the pale sunshine. "Please?"
"So long as you keep an eye on the weather,"
  said Mother Mouse.
"I'm sure more rain is on the way."

Molly and her brothers
and sister scampered across
the fields. They chased each other round
hawthorn trees, frothing white with blossom.

They hopped through
carpets of bluebells.

They were enjoying themselves
so much that they didn't notice
it was suddenly getting darker.

A large drop of rain fell on Molly's nose – and another, and then another. Big black clouds filled the sky, and the rain started to fall faster and faster. "We'll never get home in time," groaned Molly. "Where can we shelter until it stops?"

Just then, a squirrel hurried by on her
way home. She stopped when she saw
the wet little mice. Her own family were
all tucked up safe and warm in her nest.
She couldn't possibly leave the mice
out in the rain.

"Come with me," she said.
"You can shelter at my place."

Squirrel ran ahead and bounded
up a tree, but the mice didn't follow.
"Your house is too high and it doesn't
look safe in this storm," sighed Molly.

An old harvest mouse popped
her head out from under some leaves.
"You can stay with me," she said kindly,
"I have a nice warm nest of twigs."

Harvest Mouse scuttled to her home, but
the mice didn't follow. They could see that
her woven nest was far too small for them all.

"You can come to our place," cried a little rabbit,
"and join my baby brothers and sisters in the
warmth of our burrow." She couldn't leave
these poor little mice out in the storm.

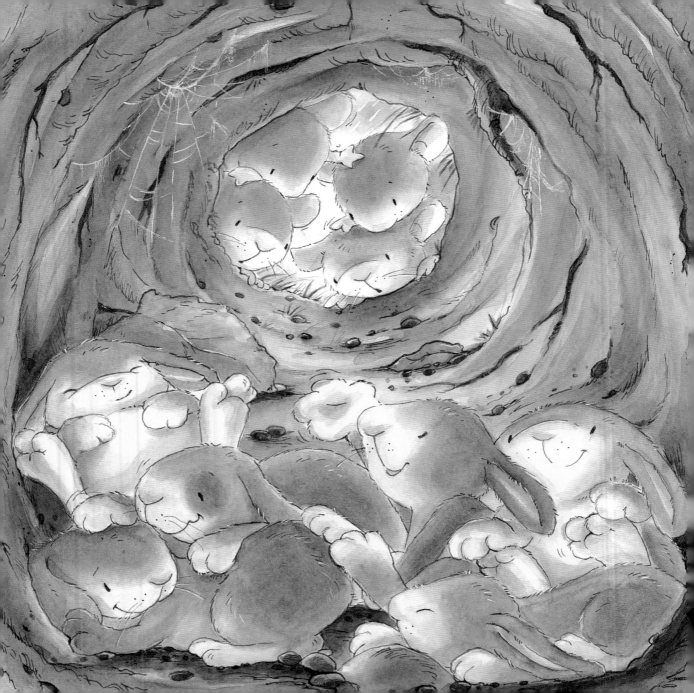

Rabbit popped down the rabbit hole, but the mice stayed outside. "Your home is very full," said Molly, peering inside at all the baby rabbits. "I think we'd all be too squashed."

Before Rabbit had time to answer, they both heard someone calling. Molly pricked her ears. "It's Mother Mouse!" she squeaked.

"Thank goodness I've found you!"
cried Mother Mouse. "The storm
is getting worse. But there's
an old hollow oak tree nearby
where we can shelter until
the rain stops."

The hollow oak tree stood at the top of
a slope. The mice scrambled inside and
were soon warm and dry.
"We'll stay here tonight," said Mother
Mouse. "You can all curl up together
and go to sleep."

But Molly couldn't sleep. She lay listening
to the roar of the wind and the lashing of
the rain, and she was worried about her
new friends. Would Harvest Mouse's home
be destroyed? Surely Rabbit's burrow would
be flooded, and Squirrel's nest blown away?
Molly looked at her family, sleeping snugly. She
couldn't leave her friends out in the storm.

Molly hurried outside. The wind tugged and
pulled at her as she struggled across the field.
There, huddled under a swaying tree,
was Squirrel.
"You must come with me,"
said Molly. "We've found
the perfect shelter."

Just then, looking tired and bedraggled, the
old harvest mouse appeared out of the grass.
"Can I come too?" she asked.
"Of course," said Molly.

As they made their way back,
they passed Rabbit and
her family huddled
under a hedge. "You'll
be nice and warm if
you come with us,"
said Molly.

At last Molly and her new friends reached the shelter of the old oak tree. Outside, the wind battered the trees and flattened the grasses. But inside, everyone was safe and dry.

The wind had dropped by the time morning came,
and as the sun crept up into the sky the friends
crawled out of their burrow. There before them was
a rainbow, stretching as far as the eye could see.

"It's for you, Molly," whispered the old harvest mouse.
"It's a special present for saving us."
And Molly smiled happily, surrounded by her family
and all her new friends.

Glitter
Greeting Cards

by Jo Packham

Mud Puddle Books
NEW YORK

Glitter Greeting Cards
by Jo Packham

Published by
Mud Puddle Books, Inc.
54 W. 21st Street
Suite 601
New York, NY 10010
info@mudpuddlebooks.com

ISBN: 978-1-59412-190-6

Printed in China.

table of Contents

Chapter 1:
Designer Tips, Techniques, and Secrets

Chapter 2:
Glitter Cards to Make and Give

Chapter 3:
Don't Forget the Envelope!

Introduction

Glitz, Glam, and Bling... What are they?

Glitz: flashy, gaudy, showy to the point of being ostentatious.

Glam: razzle-dazzle, sparkle, pizzazz, desirability, pretty, magic, delightful, alluring, charming, romantic, exciting.

Bling: hip-hop term for expensive jewelry and other pricy, attention-getting accoutrements.

Glitz, glam, and bling are all the definition of glitter: glistening, glamorous, brilliant, and showy.

Glitter is all that we love and is great fun to use. It adds that extra ordinary, over-the-top touch, and makes everything look fabulous. It will soon be your favorite thing to do!

You are about to enter a designer's world of glitter, glitz, glam, and just plain fun. After a project or two, absolutely everything will look just too plain and pedestrian if there isn't any sparkle.

Welcome to the world of glitter!

All About Glitter

Glitter is a great way to add flash and flair to cards, gifts and everything. There are a variety of glitters to choose from.

Coarse glitter: The larger bits of coarse glitter are much easier to see than fine glitter. Coarse glitter does not stick to glue very well, and does not provide as much coverage as fine glitter. It can be used by itself or mixed with fine glitter for better coverage.

Glitter glue: This type of glitter comes in a tube and is good for writing or drawing finer lines. It does not completely cover large surfaces. As glitter glue is "wet," using too much will cause your paper to wrinkle.

Fine glitter: The individual pieces of very fine glitter cannot be seen after the glitter has been applied. This is the best type of glitter for card making. It adheres well to the glue and covers completely.

Glass glitter: The oldest form of glitter, glass glitter is actually made from glass. It is available in both coarse and fine, and will tarnish after application

Designer Secrets for Glitter

While working with glitter is fun, remember that it goes everywhere! A small amount of preparation and care will help you prevent finding glitter everywhere forever. Here are a few tips for keeping those shiny bits contained!

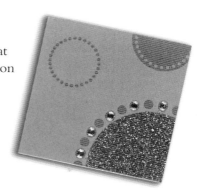

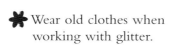Wear old clothes when working with glitter.

Pick a work surface that can be easily cleaned. Cover it with brown kraft or scratch paper. Do not use newspaper. The black print will rub off onto your cards.

Have a "Glitter Getter" and a sheet of plain paper available for each color glitter. When glittering a project, a great deal of glitter is poured onto the project but only a small amount actually adheres to glue. A Glitter Getter will help you pour leftover glitter back into container. This way, a small container of glitter will last for many many projects. To make a Glitter Getter, see instructions on page 21.

When you are finished using one color glitter, pour excess back into container immediately and replace lid. This will prevent glitter from spilling or spreading everywhere when not in use.

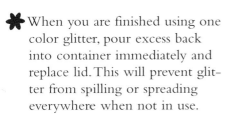

When finished glittering, wash your hands with soap and water.

5

WHITE

COPPER

ROSE

GREEN

COMBINATION
COLOR

COMBINATION
COLOR

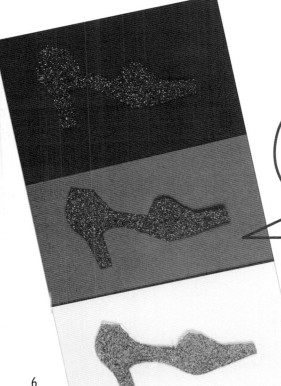

Designer Technique: Shading with Glitter

1. Try "shading" by simply using two or more colors of glitter.

2. Lightly sprinkle the first color onto the glue or adhesive.

3. Sprinkle the second color onto the glue, then repeat with additional desired colors.

4. Make certain not to "pour" the glitter onto the glue, or the remaining glitter colors will not adhere.

Designer Note: Try not to create definite lines with one color of glitter, as this will cause the second color to meet the line of the first color, not blend with it.

A Card for All Occasions

There are a number of reasons to send someone a card. Holidays, birthdays, or just to let someone know you're thinking of them. Here are a few ideas to get you started:

Holidays: Valentine's Day, Saint Patrick's Day, Easter, Mother's Day, Father's Day, Independence Day, Halloween, Thanksgiving, Hanukkah, Christmas, New Year's

Special Occasions:
birthdays, engagements, weddings, new babies, anniversaries

Designer Tip:
Not all greeting cards need to have words on the front or inside. If you want to be certain the card recipient knows exactly what message you're trying to convey, then using words are necessary. However, if you want the receiver to create their own meaning, then not using any words may be best.

Miscellaneous:
congratulations (new job, new home, receipt of an award), graduation, moving away, breaking up, meeting someone new, thank you, encouragement, friendship, apology, sickness, a loss

Designer Tip:

The same card design may be used with different sentiments or for various occasions. For example, everyone loves flowers. Plus they are fun and easy to make from paper, wood, foam shapes, or buttons. They can be plain or patterned; big or small; have centers that are glittered, beaded, buttoned, or shaped with stars, hearts, squares, or triangles.

Thanks a Bunch!

From all of us

If you were a flower, I'd pick you!

Roses are red, violets are blue, these flowers are here because I love you!

A Style All their Own

There are a number of reasons to send the cards you make, and lots of different kinds of people to receive them! All of the people in your life like different things. Here is a list of the types of cards to choose from to make for family and friends that have a style all their own.

Campy: overdone, stylish, mod, hip, clever, perceptive, sophisticated, cosmopolitan, theatrical, exaggerated, extravagant

What to Say:

♥ Passion for Fashion

♥ This is not a dress rehearsal

♥ It's a Jungle out there

Cute: delightfully pretty, dainty, created to charm, precious, childlike, delicate, enchanting, darling, joyful, cheerful, enjoyable, pleasing

What to Say:

★ A moment in my arms. Forever in my heart.

★ Sweet Dreams, Sleep Tight, I Love You, Good Night.

★ twinkle twinkle little star, do you know How loved you are?

Elegant: luxurious, posh, grand, rich, gorgeous, ornamental, excellent, superior, exquisite, tasteful, well-made, sophisticated, stylish, fashionable, cultured, lovely, classical

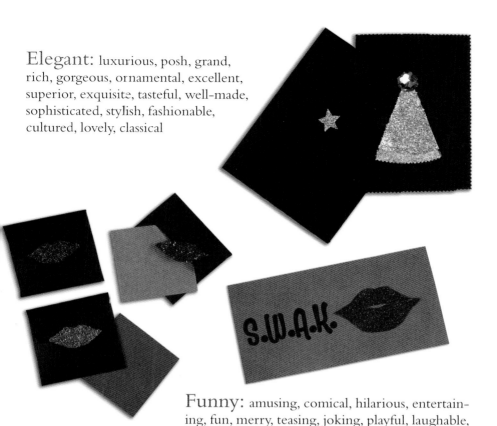

Funny: amusing, comical, hilarious, entertaining, fun, merry, teasing, joking, playful, laughable, witty, clever, saucy, sassy, curious, peculiar

Inspirational/Motivational: encouragement, spirit, passion, zeal, enthusiasm, excitement, bright, warm, assuring, comforting, spirit, support, strength, insightful, teaching

What to Say:

✸ TAKE FLIGHT!

✸ go where you want to go, be what you want to be.

✸ There is no such thing as an ordinary life

11

Pretty: pleasing, delightful, lovely, attractive, dainty, delicate, graceful, beautiful

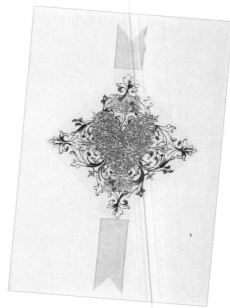

Sentimental: emotional, tender, affectionate, loving, sympathetic, compassionate, romantic, nostalgic

Under the weather?

Serious: thoughtful, pensive, reflective, sincere, honest, genuine, real, important, significant, momentous, critical

Basic Materials

Adhesive: A variety of adhesives are used in the projects found in this book. These are: glitter glue; regular white glue that dries clear; glue dots and glue strips (used in scrapbooking); mounting adhesive for projects with large areas of glitter; double-stick tape; transparent tape; specialty glues for foam, metal, or wood; and a small hot-glue gun.

Designer Tips for Adhesives:

⭐ Use glue that dries clear so that it cannot be seen through glitter.

⭐ Make sure the tip of your glue bottle is the proper width for the design being drawn. A fine-tip bottle, a small paintbrush or toothpick are best for thin lines and small dots; a medium-tipped bottle is best for thicker lines and medium to large dots; and a flat paintbrush is best for large areas.

⭐ Practice drawing with the glue bottle before you begin applying glue to artwork.

⭐ If you make a mistake when applying glue, use a cotton swab to clean glue from surface, or scrape with small piece of cardstock. Allow to dry, then begin again. If glue leaves a visible mark, you will have to extend glittered area, cover with an embellishment, or begin project again.

⭐ Remember that it is very difficult to draw a perfect line when using glue. If you desire perfection, try using double-stick tape, mounting adhesive, or strips of sticker paper to adhere glitter to paper. Double-stick adhesive strips are available in a variety of widths and sizes, and can be found in the adhesives or scrapbooking section of your local craft store.

Glitter Getter: A Glitter Getter is the perfect tool for catching excess glitter and an easy cleanup! (See page 21)

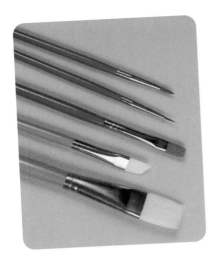

Miscellaneous: Cotton swabs; mechanical pencil with an eraser; brown kraft paper; paper towels a hole punch; wire cutters; and ribbons, threads, or strings for tags will also be called for throughout this book.

Paintbrushes: A variety of sizes of inexpensive watercolor or art brushes are necessary for applying adhesive and to brush away excess glitter from your card or envelope.

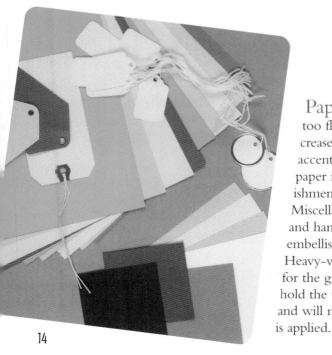

Paper: Regular-weight paper is too flimsy for a card base but it creases easily and makes nice accents for cards. Medium-weight paper is great for making embellishments and envelopes.

Miscellaneous patterned, decorative, and handmade paper all make great embellishments for beautiful cards. Heavy-weight or cardstock is used for the greeting card body. It will hold the weight of glued-on objects and will not easily wrinkle when glue is applied.

Ruler: A clear ruler is the easiest ruler to use for making glitter cards but any ruler will work.

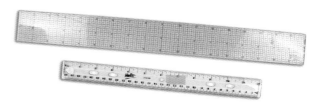

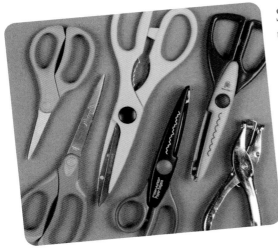

Scissors: Scissors are used for trimming cards to size and for cutting embellishments. You will need very small, pointed scissors; sharp small-sized paper scissors, sharp medium-sized paper scissors; and decorative-edged scissors, such as those used for scrapbooking.

Designer Note: Paper scissors are simply scissors used specifically for cutting paper.

Mechanical Pencil: Mechanical pencils are best because the lead is very fine and always sharp. The fine lead breaks easily, which will prevent you from applying too much pressure and making the line too dark or causing an indentation on the paper where the pencil mark is.

Designer Tip:
Always use a pencil to create cutting or placement marks. This way, the lines can be erased so they are not seen on the finished project, and the pencil marks will be much easier to see on darker papers.

Folding Cards

Today cards come in almost every size from tiny gift enclosures to oversized "big" cards. You can choose to make your cards whatever size you want to because it is so easy to make an envelope to match. If you do not wish to make your own envelope then you should choose your envelope first and make your card to fit.

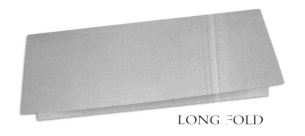

LONG FOLD

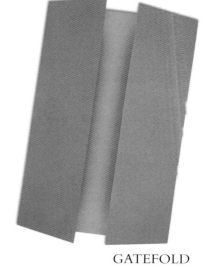

GATEFOLD

ACCORDION FOLD

Designer Note: remember if your card is oversized the envelope may take a larger piece of paper than 8½" x 11" so make certain you can find matching paper large enough to create an envelope. In this case you may wish to make a nontraditional envelope without flaps.

SHORT FOLD

16

Designer Technique: Folding Your Card

1. Measure card using a ruler and lightly pencil a mark at center.

2. Place ruler so one long edge is on marked line. Fold one edge of paper over to meet opposite side, matching up corners and holding in place with your middle and index fingers. Place your thumbs in middle of card and crease.

   Note: Make certain the fold is tight against ruler. Press down to reinforce the crease working from center of card out to edges.

3. Smooth each fold by sliding a pencil or bone folder over crease. If using a pencil, erase any unwanted marks.

Designer Technique for Basic Glitter Cards

The basics needed to make even the simplest of cards:

♥ Folded cardstock of choice

♥ Embellishments of choice

♥ Matching envelope

1. Adhere design to card front.
2. Decide areas of design to glitter. *Follow Steps 2–6 for each individual color.*

IMPORTANT: *Designer Note: If using glue in more than one area, apply different colors of glitter to glued areas one at a time, allowing glue with one color of glitter to dry thoroughly before covering additional areas with glue and adding next color of glitter. For example: apply glue or adhesives to all copper areas, glitter, and let dry. Next apply glue and adhesives to all green areas, glitter, and let dry.*

If you decide not to let the glue dry between the glittering of second, third, or more colors the glitter colors may mix together on the design. If you do not wait for glue to dry between colors be careful not to smear wet glue with your hand while gluing and glittering additional areas and do not shake off excess glitter into "Glitter Getter" (see page 21) until all colors of glitter have been applied and the glue has dried. This excess glitter in "Glitter Getter" will be mixed and if there are multiple colors combined it may not be able to be used again.

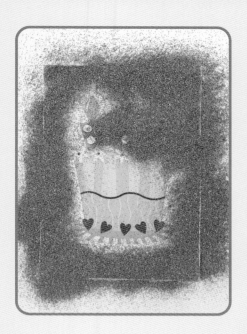

3. Cover larger areas with double-stick tape or mounting adhesive and add glue or adheasive dots in areas where you will be using the same color glitter. Place design on "Glitter Getter" and apply glitter.

Designer Note: Larger, flatter areas should be completed first.

4. Adhere glue dots to smaller areas of design. Do not remove protective backing until ready to glitter. Remove backing and glitter.

5. Using a tube or bottle of glue, trace lines or "color in" remaining areas that are to be glittered. (Remember to do this step one color at a time.) Placing your hand against your work surface will help keep it steady. *Note: Begin at the top, left-hand side of page and work your way down and to the right in order to prevent smudging adhesive that has already been applied.*

6. Allow glue to dry. Repeat Steps 2–6 for all remaining colors.

Glitter Idea #1

Glitter Idea #2

Glitter Idea #3

Designer technique for Making a "Glitter Getter"

This is a simple but very important tool when work-ing with glitter. Use a separate Glitter Getter for each color of glitter, and a second sheet of medium weight paper to place under each Glitter Getter.

1. Fold an 8½" x 11", or larger, sheet of paper in half, crease fold. Unfold and lay paper flat on work surface with the crease side down.

2. Apply adhesive to design, place project on Glitter Getter and sprinkle glitter. Leave project on Glitter Getter until adhesive dries.

3. Pick up project and shake off excess glitter.

4. Pick up the sides of Glitter Getter so that glitter falls into the fold.

5. Place edge of crease into glitter container and pour in glitter. Tap the back of Glitter Getter to remove any glitter that may stick to paper. If you miss container and glitter spills, it will fall onto second sheet of medium weight paper. Now pour this spilled glitter back into Glitter Getter.

Embellish!

Cards can be embellished any way you wish. Use your imagination—the sky is the limit!

Scrapbooking supplies: such as rivets; letters and words of all types; charms; stickers; die-cuts; dimensional sticker images; beads; wire, wood, and foam shapes; ribbons; rhinestones; rubber stamps; and almost anything else you find in the scrapbooking aisle can all be used to embellish your cards.

Party supply stores, dollar stores, and super centers all have hundreds of items that can be used in cardmaking. Use your imagination: swizzle sticks can be glittered and glued to a card; confetti can be placed inside the card envelope for added surprise; and small candies can add a sweet treat for the recipient of your card.

Cut-outs

When applying embellishments decide which glue is best for the job. Directions on the adhesive bottle or package will give you the information that you need.

Embellishments

Create

Stickers

23

Applying Embellishments

The type of embel-
lishment that is
applied will dictate
the manner in which
it is adhered – glue,
glue dots, mounting
adhesive, etc.

IMPORTANT
Designer Note:
Adult supervision
may be required
when using
wire cutters.

A number of
fun buttons can be
used to spice up your
design. Flat buttons can be
glued, or sewn to card using
pre-made holes. Shank buttons
are the kind with a small piece on
the back. For the purpose of card
making, you will need to remove the
shank. It can then be adhered with white
glue, a glue gun, or glue dots.

Metal, paper, plastic, foam, or wooden numbers, letters, and words are great ways to embellish your cards.

Designer Tip: If you want the buttons to lie flat, use white glue, glue dots or strips, double-stick tape, sticker sheets, or mounting adhesive. If you want embellishments to have a three-dimensional, or raised, effect, use foam glue dots.

Designer Tip: Use the technique on page 24 for removing the back of buttons with other embellishments such as silk flowers, swizzle sticks, and shaped rivets.

Oh So Easy Glitter Cards

Sometimes you just need a fast easy card that is extraordinary. They are fun to think about, to shop for, and oh so simple to make. Buy a non-traditional card embellishment that represents what it is that you want to say, add glitter, glue it to the card front, write a message......or not, and give it away. With a little creativity, your ideas will be endless!

What to say:

* ❋ You make everything add up
* ❋ I Love You X Infinity
* ❋ You are my #1

What to say:

* ❋ Congratulations for Crossing the Finish Line!
* ❋ TRADING PAINT
* ❋ Start Your Engines
* ❋ Need for Speed

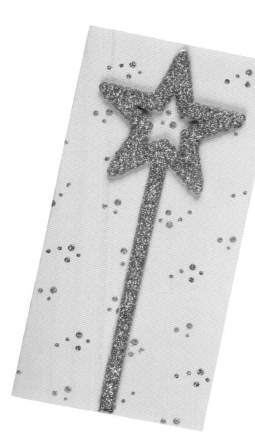

What to say:

⭐ Make a Wish

⭐ Celebrate the Magic

⭐ A Wishing Wand for You

⭐ She changes everything
   she touches

What to say:

💜 What Color is Imagination?

💜 Color me shades of
   blue..... without YOU!

💜 for memory has painted
   this perfect day with
   colors that never fade
   (by carrie jacobs bond)

What to say:

♥ **You're #1**

♥ SweeT 16

♥ I Love 50!

♥ **It's Crazy to be 8!**

♥ LucKY #7

Designer Tip
Use playing cards or pre-school flip cards and pick the numbers that are perfect for the occasion.

What to say:

❋ If not now when?

❋ Where have you been?

❋ I'm Confused!

❋ Whatever the question is, the answer is no (yes)!

❋ Just because!

❋ Why Not?

❋ Have I ever told you.........

28

What to say:

✻ When will you ever have more time than you do right now?

✻ I HAD THE TIME OF MY LIFE!

✻ There is no time like the present

✻ tHis day will neveR come tHis way again

✻ TIME IS PRECIOUS, SPEND IT WISELY!

✻ Only time will tell

✻ when was the last time you did something for the first time?

What to say:

✿ Celebrate. It's Your Day!

✿ I'm Worth It!

✿ It's Good Being #1

✿ QUEEN FOR A DAY

Designer Tip:
Buy a blue ribbon at a party supply or novelty store, glitter the ribbon tails, then add a pin back. This is a great way to say, "You're number one!"

Celebrate Every Moment

What to say:

⭐ Make a Wish

⭐ Wish Big

⭐ It's birthday Time

What to say:

* ❋ Stay Focused

* ❋ Hey Good Looking!

* ❋ Looking for
  Mr. Right...now!

* ❋ is it true you have to see it to believe it or
  do you have to believe it before you can see it

Close your eyes

so you can see

By the book

What to say:

* ♥ Your Story Begins Here

* ♥ Read all about it

The Search for Buried treasure

A treasure hunt is a fun activity for kids and adults alike—invite your friends to a treasure hunt by creating specially monogrammed cards with their first initial on the front and the party details on the inside.

Create "treasure clues" by glittering the cards that contain the clues and hiding them inside miniature treasure chests. Use white glue to cover desired areas of the treasure chests with glitter.

What to say:

✱ I'm glad I "found" you!

✱ Ahoy! Keep yer eye on the loot!

✱ You're a Treasure to Me

Fanfare of Fortune

A sweet gift that anyone can enjoy is a glitzy take-out box of fortune cookies! Simply glitter the designs of your choice, such as hearts and flowers in bright colors, and adhere them to the box. Embellish a card with the same designs, and tuck inside the box before adding the cookies.

If desired, create more glittery shapes and adhere to a brightly colored fan. Crease the shapes so that they bend with the fan folds.

Designer Tip:
This project also makes a great invitation to a party. Simply tuck an invitation card into the box with the phrase "Accept the Next Proposal You Receive" or "Luck Will Visit You on ......" put the date of the party

What to say:

★ Great Fortune Will Soon Be Yours...

★ Happy times await you

★ Good Luck Is On Its Way

★ You Will Be Famous One Day

★ from a past misfortune good luck will come to you

Mardi Gras Masquerade

Mardi Gras means fun, celebration, and
partying. Simply coat plastic masks
in glitter and attach a small
tag as a card or party
invitation.

Designer Tip:
If you are using regular-sized
cards or invitations, try slipping
some Mardi Gras beads into the
envelope for an added,
festive touch.

What to say:

❋ Celebrate!

❋ It's Party Time!

An accordion folded tag with glittered picture frames makes a great party favor. Supply small cameras so that friends can take pictures of each other. On the card glue a frame to first tag then leave every other tag side blank and attach a glittered frame to facing tag.

Guests can add pictures from the party to frames and write in memories of their favorite party moments. Just remember to use light-colored or metallic felt tip pens. Finish off by punching a hole through the top of the tag, and tie with string, ribbon, or Mardi Gras beads.

Designer Tip:
For picture frames adhere bottom and sides to it, but leave top open so a photograph can be slipped easily inside.

Caliente Fiesta!

This card is simple to make but so much fun to receive!
Cut designs from paper before glittering, or purchase
swizzle sticks and cut ends off. Use a paintbrush to
apply glue before glittering. Spice up your party
decorations with even more glitter, and you're
off to a sizzling start.

What to say:

★ You're hot!

★ Party On!

★ VERRRRY HOT!

★ caliente fiesta!

★ shake things up!

Designer Tip:
To ensure glitter stays adhered
to decorations, try spritzing
them with hairspray.

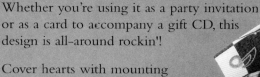

Disco Mania

Whether you're using it as a party invitation or as a card to accompany a gift CD, this design is all-around rockin'!

Cover hearts with mounting adhesive and apply glitter. Include record stickers, shimmery disco balls, or any other desired embellishments!

What to say:

♥ Let's Dance

♥ You Rock!

♥ Do The hustle

♥ And the Beat Goes On...

♥ Another One Bites the Dust

♥ I've Got You Babe

Lucky #7

These fun and fabulous cards are the perfect way to say, "It's your lucky day!" Just glitter the center of three poker chips, or "frame" a playing card with Vegas-worthy glitz.

What to say:
* Lucky You!
* Good Luck!
* It's Your Lucky Day!
* I'm Lucky You Are My Friend

38

You are #1

Anyone that plays sports will appreciate a good luck card before the big game. Glam up your desired slogan with the same color glitter as the recipient's sports team, and make the inside just as sporty with stickers, ribbons, or any other embellishments.

What to say:

* It ain't over til it's over!
* Take me out to the ballgame
* Practice, Practice, Practice
* girls just want to win!
* The secret to stardom is the rest of the team
  (by John Wooden)
* The desire and the will must be stronger than the skill

Hollywood

Want to let someone know they're a star in your life or invite your friends to watch the Oscars? Invite them with an invitation to see the stars! This card says it all.

Designer Note: Stickers, wooden or foam shapes die cuts, or cutout hearts and stars can all be glittered.

What to say:

- ★ Star Power
- ★ Star Struck
- ★ YOU ARE A STAR
- ★ "Where Are You Going?" I asked;
  "To Dance Among the Stars," she said.
- ★ Party With the Stars
- ★ Wish upon a star

40

Princess

This simple card can be embellished to your royal heart's content! Just adhere glitter to foam, wood, or paper shapes before applying shapes to front of card.

What to say:

♥ Queen Me!

♥ Life is Good!

♥ Me, Me, Me!

♥ Princess of quite a lot

♥ Some Days You Just Feel Like a Princess

♥ It's Good to Be Queen

♥ It's a Queen Thing

♥ Everyday is a Tiara Day!

Designer Tip:
For an extra touch, glue jewels to the points of the crown.

Gifts Galore

Cut a series of squares, making each subsequent square .6 cm smaller than the one preceding it. Glitter each square a different color and adhere to card. Adhere ribbon from top to bottom and from left to right as shown in photograph, finishing with a bow on top.

What to say:

❋ DREAM BIG

❋ You Are a Gift We Celebrate All Year

❋ Good Friends Make Good Gifts

❋ Everyone Has a Gift to Give

❋ Give Me Everything I Want and Nothing I Need

❋ I Want It all and i Want It Delivered

❋ Happy Happy Birthday to My Dear Friend

You Light Up My Life

Cutting strips of co-coordinating paper in different size widths and lengths makes this card of candles. Use different sizes of double stick tape to adhere strips, glitter whichever candles and flames you like.

What to say:

❀ Memories are simply moments that refuse to be ordinary

❀ How old would you be if you didn't know how old you were?

Shop 'til you drop!

These tiny shopping bags can be cut from plain or printed papers, adhere a handle made from string or thread, and then add glitter.

iT's in The Bag!

What to say:

♥ caRRied away?!

♥ too much of everything is never enough!

♥ Gotta Have It!
   Want It!
   Need It!

♥ Retail Therapy

♥ Let's Shop!

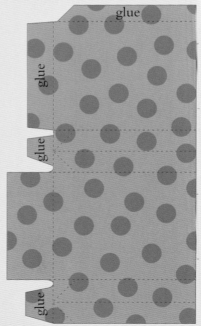

glue

glue

glue

glue

Actual size

A Gift for You

Be Everyone You Are!

The clothing patterns used in this design can be funky, fun, or fancy; kitschy or traditional; for adults, teens, or babies... Just use your imagination!

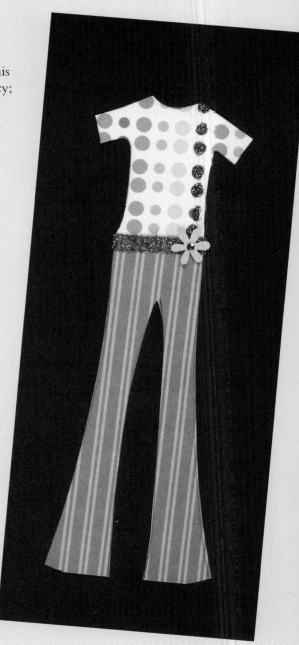

What to say:

* Trust Yourself
* The Life You Lead Should Be the Life You Love
* Live Like You Mean It!
* Elegance Is an Attitude!
* When Was the Last Time You Did Something for the First Time?
* What do you pack to pursue your dreams and what do you leave behind?

DESIGNER TIP:
A fun touch for this card is to
extend the skirt or the pant legs down
past the bottom edge of card. Make
certain your envelope is large enough
to accommodate design
without bending it.

47

Call of the Wild!

Some say, "You are what you wear!" and even though that may not always be true, your clothes can definitely speak a thousand words about what you like and who you are. So if you want to change your life for a day, change your clothes….especially your shoes! Now, you can be anyone you want to be.

Card Phrases:

⭐ Everything is Sweetened by Risk (by Alexander Smith)

⭐ The world of reality has its limits, the world of imagination is boundless. (by Rousseau)

⭐ "Goodbye", she said, "I'm off to join the CIRCUS! (by Leigh Standley)

Party Hats

These party hats make a great invitation or thank you card for a party recently attended. Just draw hat pattern to the desired size, cut and fold pattern on dotted line, then glitter!

Designer Tip:
Top the hats with a pom-pom, rhinestone, or button.

Card Phrases:

⭐ It's Party Time!

⭐ Celebrate! It's Your Day

Attach pom-pom

Hat pattern

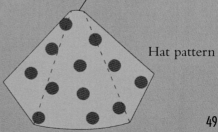

Rim pattern

49

Purseonality!

What is a girl without her purse?! We all want more than one, we all need more than one, we all have to have more than one!

Card Phrases:

❀ You're Worth It!

❀ the day you were born the world had to make room for a little more fancy (by Leigh Standley)

❀ YOU GO GIRL!

❀ sHOPPORTUNIST!

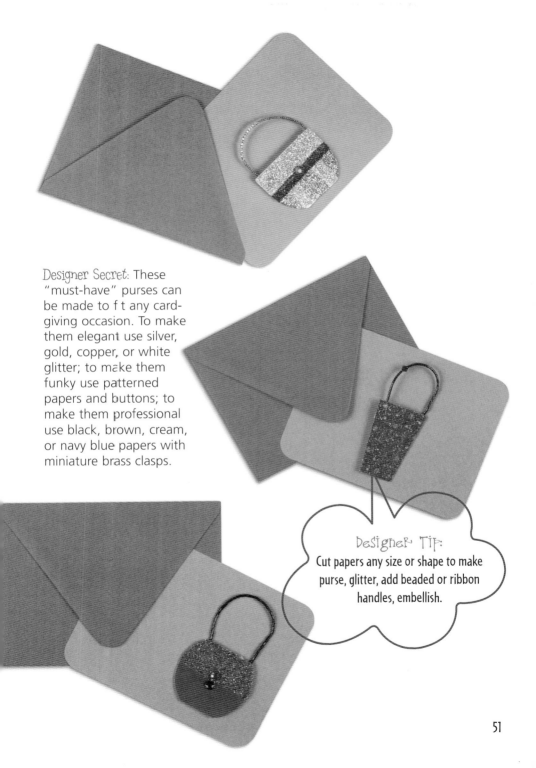

Designer Secret: These "must-have" purses can be made to f t any card-giving occasion. To make them elegant use silver, gold, copper, or white glitter; to make them funky use patterned papers and buttons; to make them professional use black, brown, cream, or navy blue papers with miniature brass clasps.

Designer Tip:
Cut papers any size or shape to make purse, glitter, add beaded or ribbon handles, embellish.

Bee Yourself!

Did you know that according to the principles of aerodynamics bees shouldn't be able to fly? No one ever told them they couldn't do it, so they just do!

Card Phrases:

❋ Beelieve

❋ Bee Everything You Are

❋ Bee Happy!

❋ Thank you for beeing my friend

❋ Beelieve in Yourself

❋ Bee a Dreamer

❋ JUST BEELIEVE

English Cracker Cards

These "crackers" are tubes that can hold a scroll card as well as a tiny treasure. In Victorian times, crackers were given at Christmas parties and contained a charm, a joke, and a tissue paper crown. When the ends were pulled, a friction spot on the inside would snap, creating the cracking noise. While our crackers will not make a noise, as the snaps are difficult to find, they are still fun to make, fun to give, and fun to receive!

Designer Technique:

1. Measure the length of a toilet paper tube, adding 2" (5cm) to each end.

2. Measure the circumference of the tube, add 2" (5cm).

3. Using dimensions, cut two layers of brightly colored plain paper.

4. Cover tissue paper tube with strips of double-stick tape.

5. Place a line of double-stick tape down long edge of cut paper.

6. Place paper tube onto paper opposite line of double-stick tape. Roll paper onto tube, smoothing as you go.

7. Tie one end with string or ribbon. Fill cracker with desired objects, then tie the other end.

8. Glitter crackers.

Stepping Out

The mood of this fashion-forward card will be changed depending on the paper you choose to use. Glitter against black paper will make this look like a party shoe, while brown paper creates more of a business shoe. Yellow paper with pink flowers will create a summer shoe perfect for a luncheon invitation. The shoe on this card can be made to match just about any occasion you can think of!

Something Old, Something New, Something Borrowed... and Great Shoes!

Designer Tip: The star on this card is cut from vellum—be careful when adhering vellum, because, as too much glue or glue dots will show through. Simply place the glue behind the glitter to avoid unsightly spots.

Card Phrases:

⭐ One Shoe Can Change Your Life...by Cinderella

⭐ i'm late, i'm late for a very important date!

⭐ Lost: one glass slipper by Cinderella

⭐ SOME DAYS YOU JUST HAVE TO DANCE

⭐ Put on your dancing shoes

⭐ Here is to world peace and cute shoes

It's Your Lucky Day!

Card Phrases:

* ✳ Find Your Own Luck

* ✳ Best of Luck!

* ✳ The harder you work
  the luckier you get

Two Hearts, One Love

Hearts, every time you see one it
is like seeing it for the first time!

Card Phrases:

* ♥ 1 + 1 = US

* ♥ I will love you forever,
  for always

* ♥ Forever Us

* ♥ My heart reminds me

* ♥ Love is in the air

* ♥ This is where I belong

* ♥ Love you, sooo much

* ♥ Friend to Friend,
  Heart to Heart

Ready-Made tags

These tags are so simple; you can make them in minutes. Purchase a tag or card from your favorite store, spice it up with glitter and embellish-ments!

Designer Tip:
Make a cute beaded ring for the envelope by taking a thin piece of wire, string plastic beads, and twist the ends of wire together.

Mirror, Mirror On The Wall

In Victorian times men put tiny mirrors in the cards that they gave to their lady friends so that she could "see" who he loved. Today, cute cards with mirrors can be given by anyone, to anyone, for any reason.

Card Phrases:

❀ You Go Girl!

❀ It's all about me!

❀ More than a pretty face

❀ Mirror, mirror on the wall. I am my mother after all!

❀ Smile, it confuses people.

❀ Let me be the princess!

❀ When you believe in yourself, everything is possible.

❀ Be yourself, everyone else is taken.

Designer Tip:
Small round, square, or oval mirrors can be found in craft and hobby stores. To make this card put a ribbon down the middle of the page using double stick tape, cut out a crown, glitter, adhere with dimensional glue dot, add a mirror, and write your message.

Imagine

Not all cards have to be traditional. This one is a small book that can be used as a sketchbook, scrapbook, or a storybook.

Designer Tip:
Make the inside of your card as "pretty" as the outside. When you tape a picture on the inside, frame it with paper, ribbon, or glitter so there are no raw edges showing.

Designer Technique:

1. To make a 4"-square book, cut pages 4" x 8". Stack pages together, fold and crease in half. Make the cover by cutting cardstock to ½" larger than the book pages on all sides. Cut square, or other desired shape, in center of cover. Staple cover and pages together along crease line. Glitter border on cut window of card front by using strips of double-stick tape.

2. Fit desired photograph behind opening, adhere using tape, finish edges. Write desired message on first page, and fit into matching envelope.

Chapter 3

Don't Forget the Envelope!

Envelopes are the frosting on the cake, the finishing touch, the *pièce de résistance!* Sometimes, the envelope can be as important as the card. It is the first "word" of your message, which renders a plain, white envelope beneath you!

Designer Technique:

Here are a few basics for creating envelopes as fabulous as your cards:

1. Measure card and add ¼" to 1" on all sides. If there are embellish-ments that will push the envelope outward, make certain to accommodate for this with a larger envelope.

2. Lightly sketch outline for envelope onto the center of a sheet of medium-weight paper. Add one flap for each side, as well as top and bottom flaps. See diagram for inspiration!

3. Cut out shape.

4. Fold and crease flaps, using ruler as a guide.

5. Apply glue strips, double-stick tape, or adhesive to small side flaps. Fold and smooth. Repeat with bottom flap.

6. Decorate envelope as desired.

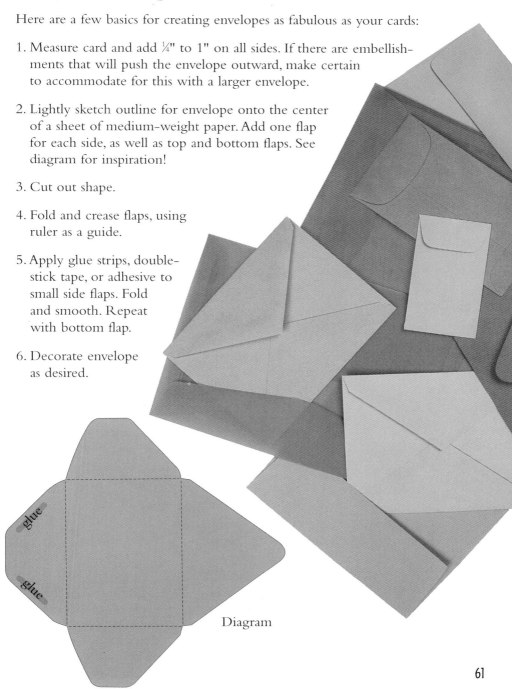

glue

glue

Diagram

XOXO

Designer Technique:

1. Cut and fold cardstock.

2. Trim edge with decorative-edged scissors, then fold and adhere flaps.

3. Punch hole and thread ribbon through as shown in photograph. Add button or bead, if desired, and tie a bow.

4 Glitter message, insert card, and voila! Your card is complete!

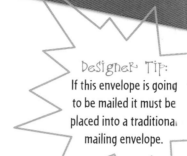

Designer Tip:
If this envelope is going to be mailed it must be placed into a traditional mailing envelope.

Party Glam tubes

These party tubes can be purchased at party supply, craft, and novelty stores. Wrap double stick tape around tubes, glitter, embellish, fill with letter rolled into a scroll, replace end cap, and give.

Designer Tip:
If these are to be mailed they will have to be placed in a mailing tube or box.

Designer Secret:
Fill tubes with the recipient's favorite candy as well as a note.

62

Let's Do Lunch!

These cute little lunch boxes can be found in party supply and novelty stores.

Glitter a large flower shape of choice. String alphabet beads to read: Let's Do Lunch on a thin wire. Make the wire long enough to thread into the back hinge and into the inside of the lunch box. Place small glue dots on the back of every other bead to hold them in place. Place invitation in lunchbox with treats, and you have an offer that nobody can refuse!

Paper Party Bags

These colorful bags can be purchased in several sizes and colors at craft, paper, or party supply stores.

Designer Technique:

1. Use die-cut butterfly, fold on dotted lines, glitter butterfly body.

2. Take a purchased pinwheel, cut stick length of bag, paint stick with glue and glitter, attach to bag with glue gun.

3. Make a small tag and envelope, punch a hole, tie with colored threads, and attach to bag. Use candle button as a closure.

IMPORTANT
Designer Note: Adult supervision may be required when using glue gun.